Archilochus on the Moon

Simon Perril

Archilochus on the Moon

Shearsman Books

First published in the United Kingdom in 2013 by
Shearsman Books
50 Westons Hill Drive
Emersons Green
BRISTOL
BS16 7DF

Shearsman Books Ltd Registered Office
30–31 St. James Place, Mangotsfield, Bristol BS16 9JB
(this address not for correspondence)

www.shearsman.com

ISBN 978-1-84861-306-5

Acknowledgements
Some of these poems have appeared in *P.N. Review, Poetry Wales, Tears in the Fence* and *Shearsman*: I thank the editors for their support and interest. I inhabited Archilochus in an earlier poem (not featured here) called 'Nettle Tongue', gathered in *A Clutch of Odes* by Oystercatcher Press.

Cover collage, from a sequence *Under Austerity Rubble Ancestral Bird-Folk lay Future Eggs*, by Simon Perril

This book is for my extended family the Demon Crew; for Mum and Dad for putting me up in their Barleythorpe garret; for the hospitality of Public Houses; for Holly and Erin (when they're older!); and for Kathleen Bell, whose belief and interest in it—and the early gift of Michael Ayrton's *Archilochus*—gave me a rhythm to work by.

"Announce to the Parians, Archilochus, that I bid you found a conspicuous city on the moon".

—The Oracle at Delphi

1.

the throat and feet collect it:
dust, deep and the colour of age
spread thick as a painted lady's cheek.

We settle on the pock-marked grave
of all faces; the undergarments
of all the sacked places
the oracle sent us to,
for a few more allotments

lands to turn our spear-flexing hands
to; and if they are taken,
Ares, there is no mistaking
with what we irrigate crops.

Yet here the seas have died
so to what, exactly, do we sacrifice
save memories of wineskins,
fair-capped waves, Parian figs
and wood-topped hills.

I offer thanks
and my arse
for a flag.

2.

we call it the Child Lands
as the thinness of air
leaves us helpless as our young

and we dream whilst awake
of mornings, trees and seas
and not to feel each frosted bone
anger the other;

this sword-work under the skin
makes the body gently sing

for we are strung out under stars,
and the sky's perpetually thick
as lust, and no less black

our chests shield-wall tight
rattle like wifely prattle;
our bird-fast hearts,
caged fists

3.

for this is the strangest island,
inked on all sides
skies bubbled
like wine too fast poured

yet the land is parched;
the only damp
is infantry crotch
and the tears of those keep watch
on the scabby hills.

Here are rocks to throw,
tho we are not spoilt for targets
despite our buffoon leader

his dragoon-speak
lacier than his locks,
flouncier than frocks

—shroud-cloths
for moon-moths
to nibble at:

we peer at the Earth
through these holes

4.

we wake wave-wet
for want of the sea,
light fires of our fish-nets

late locusts
upon a land long-stamped
by the dead, their dust-life
we swallow
along with fight-guff

the auguries are fucked. We
keep them company.

Hedgehogs
have it nailed

5.

as a whelp I swam,
felt the moon's clutch;
and now it's weak

soft as the pulse
to a flute

and disputes are similarly
distant, dance
on the wick of a lit spear tip;

for such is thought,
my nipples crack
with imaginary salt

the only measured motion
that governs here:
my bowels

6.

yet things grow
thick in the mind:
soil between our ears,

interior fields fatten
rich in putrefying matter,
the tangled roots of our years
of love and war and trade

and perhaps then it will rain
in the fitful dreams
of twitching men
on this tinder-dry plain

nothing
upon which to sharpen
my blade

7.

we beat the Thracians here
stride and stomp the desiccated straits
so many cocks

but for what else
do we roost in craters,
rot on this lunar perch?

For pockets of coins
like young hedgehogs, easy
to catch, so hard
to hold on to

save here
—no markets on the moon.
And I couldn't give a fucking fig
for there are none

8.

Zeus, a fucking sign
would be welcome, other

than your swap
of newly smith'd spears

for a spine.
Until then

I decline all offerings, place
no further bets

and if I'm still
your pet, be advised

I bite
even my own limbs;

what's mine, is yours:
a mouth full of blood

irrigates my pride,
sole lunar crop

9.

I speak ill, as
we've had our fill of Zeus-born kings
and Spartan heroes.

Sack the moon,
and you sack all
that lights the underside of Eros

stokes
those body-bits
that do the joining

and the mind
they favour and fever
riots like a market-place.

I have no love of tyranny.
Everything is for the Gods, so
they can have this:

Thanks

10.

Artemis, Selene and Hecate
you lunar three
owe me an explanation;

after this abysmal journey
to a land beyond coin and precinct
to where the Earth-stone sinks
below the horizon:

where should I find one
with whom to play
the sinews of my soft horn;

for it may yet
produce song
when skilfully played upon

still elevate
white
libations

11.

day, day, day
you stay so long here
sleep seems the wrong decision

even when, Earthshine-blind,
time itself freezes
glass discolours

and we discover
nothing soft; no waves
have played rocks
to pebbles

not a single snowflake
shapes these peaks,
yet our feet are winged

things change weight;
a thrown feather
outstrips a heavier vessel

and we no longer wrestle
with the packs on our backs
being Olympian

on this heap of stones

12.

house of holes,
land of collisions,

you rain rocks
like a battlefield

yet deal no victory,
heap no spoils.

Let's hazard Zeus knows
why he's gouged and plucked

all manner of coloured stuff
from this standing stone:

this bone pendant
swung around no neck

13.

I keep watch
in the edge rays
of the rose light

for night is welcome
like the hair of a courtesan
cast over shoulders

and back;
that pale terrain
sloping down a bony track

to meet a minor moon
and soon, its underside
of myrtle spray

14.

this business
we do with the Gods
grows strange

in this department
of calamity and punishment;
this lunar penalty

may yet see a holocaust
of pigs, if
swine can be found,

a trench dug
deep enough
in this apology for ground

with my barbed tongue

15.

O Neobulé
were you here

we'd lay
play botany

amongst the craters
I'd part petals

wet
your other mouth

and we'd talk
till nothing's

left to say

16.

before sailing
for lunar seas,
these moon-bound men

signed an oath
will bind them
to ashen coasts

till they boast
of the home banished them,
the place that will stone
their return
without barley,
coin or plot;

and later they'll sleep
on rubble beds
heads commemorative
earthenware: for hope

scares easy,
like white horses
upon a wave;

retreats
like my cock
in the cold

17.

expelled,
I act in kind
and spew,

evenly on friend and foe,
my foul mouth;
need no Pythia

to breathe vapours
and pronounce imperial capers
necessary

for the moon
is a fledgling democracy: fowl
in thin-boned structure,

scarcely fed
yet capable of flight; shits
from an unobtainable height

18.

last night I dreamt
a crater-dish of bird-bones
cast as an oracle

yet Apollo bid me
junk the outcome
and set to work;

so I stripped sticks white
in the grey sand,
binding them tight with cat-gut

to arrive at a pipe
and blew
hymns through civic holes

this low-born sound
of the body's subjects
under duress
like an ass's back

19.

the fox and rabbit
have their holes.

Spartan boys
have their military toys

sufficiently polished;
what constitution!

And after they've played away
they home with a pigeon's purpose.

There is no homecoming
from the moon:

strewn across the ground
the ashes

of my wedding feast
returned

for me to sweep

20.

Zeus of Oaths and Tithes
I remain perplexed
on this matter of sacrifice.

On Paros we'd strip an ox
back to its basic parts. Feast
on the finest portions of beast

and only as the grease
pearled in our beards
would we return thanks

in fat-wrapped thigh-bones
blistered to buggery
on your altar.

A flourishing city
honours the gods,
gives that you will give;
but do you not, Zeus
scoff at offal and bone?

On the moon we strip dignity
back to its basic parts
of bone: our new home
has no place for it
is swept away
like the rumour of seas.

What not-on-earth
appeases you, Zeus?
these thighs have little fat on them
and we don't bake
under the charred skies

though we spit
and learn this new pact:
that here the deal
is different; you
scoff the fullest meal,
leave us
hope's carcass

21.

so what
of alignments of stars

when no knuckles align
around my stick;

all of the bee
you'll find in me:

honey, wax
and sting

22.

Lycambes' ghost
visits most amongst
Mnemosyne's folk;

and the self-righteous prick
has a point
to accompany the ruff of weals
a noose makes;

but he misunderstands
the crux of song.

The butterflies in my stomach-pit
hit upon the wrong:
they are a pattern
assembled, reassembled

this riot-rhythm
is what I bottle
and the poems flutter and buzz
with the life-scuzz

23.

this rhyme
sets a trap,
wraps loose
and scattered limbs

folds them in
as the Apennine range
of the moon
holds my voice
as it exits

bounces wide
across this space
and back

I catch my breath
as once I caught
Thracian rains
mouth agape in battle

as once I caught
Pandora
unpicking the links
of my spine

and casting lots

24.

Glaucus, one who wears
his hair in horns
cannot hope
to escape my scorn.

Such play is fit
for the patterns
it pleases Zeus to shape

in a day, discard
tomorrow—He
must have sport.

I must obey
Apollo's call, Iambus' gall

25.

on Parian hills,
I'd oftimes sit, gaze

on the soft cloud
of a mid-day moon;

how its milk-skin
would ripple

the surface of my day-dreams.
Now we stand upon it,

that cloud's broken-dream statuary
of moon-sick men

whose nightside skin
is mollusc-moist,

bereft of shell.
So they bury themselves

in ash that never felt
the company of embers

26.

would that I could
accept Dionysus' counsel,
let his words
grease my speech-parts
and adjacent mechanisms.

Thus anointed
I'd gargle sweet specimens
at the fermenting skies,
whine like a desert-dog
for his bitch.

But here the only grapes
are the withered plums
of infantry men
shrunk to raisins,

and—despite the absence
of a better offer—
I'll not suck them

27.

my would-have-been
wife, at the end
of last night you left me
a word
in my waking ear:
my pet name

and I became
invertebrate:
sank through dry grey heave
into the imaginary
sea

28.

Eros unhatched
from this buckled sphere,
in lunar dispatch,
still fucks with my head-gear;

bids me patch
this cracked-pot skull
to settle certain matters:

a ghost is something
like a wife's dowry:
it follows her
though she'll never hold it.

A poem is something like a wife;
it cannot carry property,
save a personal slave or two.

A poet is something
like a ghost; gone
from this world,
granted special leave

to press their claims
from beyond—as long as they're fed
regular crap
to keep them away.

A moon is a rotten egg
offered to the dead:
a grave-jar sunk
beneath our feet

for safe-keep

29.

you can retract
your word
like a blade

and the wound puckers
proud: I
am that mouth,

talk the nonsense
pushes the insides
out

that grants
the body
shout

30.

Lycambes,
in my dreams,
your daughter's there

and when she foams
I make my presence known
hard

then wake
shaping my spear-hand
to a cup

that spills
coming like an army:
late

31.

the things I've lost
lust after me,
their former colony

tilt their tongues
to my ear-crater
and talk.

They tell how close
the most distant hope is
to dereliction;

how the moon
pockets both our gloom
and affliction
like silt
spilt on a river floor

and the more I listen,
the more I learn
what the Sybil really ranted:

how we've founded
Hecate's shrine
in the dark side of our minds
and the moon
is its dust-dappled mirror

I peer in
to catch all my actions
completed, surrounded
by what I've not done:

my life undone

32.

Glaucus, this land
has your eyes
and a First Sergeant's lies
to commend it

yet still we cannot command it
to grow
though we sow oats
solo

in crater dishes,
under twin bowls
of Earth and Sun

and the spilt stars
of Hera's milk

33.

the ship of State
has great flanks
thicker than the trunks
of Phrygian women

yet she'll not sail
these lunar seas
just yet,
despite expanding girth.

For this earth can make
no trade, except
in sleep;
and that exchange
won't temper victory coins

tho it hardens more than hearts,
and those other organs
we're no less attached to
in the nightly duress
of dream.

For my bit,
I have planted seed
and watered it
with the same instrument

34.

Hephaistus, let us
you and I
play a game: I will

make a wish
from immediate materials
chiefly bone and blood

and further soft stuff;
jam beneath the head-bone,
that joins the ears

to those daily fears we
grant shape later.
I will make this wish
substance, stand it tall
for all to survey

—if you will burn it
straight away: let Delphi
smell *those* vapours

and know
how we've prospered
lined the pock-marked pocket
of the moon

35.

all weighs less,
and less
the subtraction blue
through the absent atmosphere

yet this unthinkable place,
difficult to hold or harvest,
borrows a certain grace
when all's air-borne

and the light breeze
of fifty sleeping men
gently handles
my extremities;

then the moon's
a dead seed-head
planted in each skull-cup:

petition Demeter
softly
for a wet spell

36.

one night as a kid
in the country—Lissides—
these lunar auguries
came to a head.

As I led a cow
across the soil-black night
to market, I was met
by a gaggle of women

laughed like surf
on rock, bent
my ears like barley
under breeze;

and these ladies
wanted more than bull,
but bartered for the beast
anyways,

till there came as a sudden
the strangest swap:
dropped at my feet
under the butter-beams,
a lyre,

and my father's ire and doubt
at this outcome
saw him run the island out
in pursuit of cow;

pushed him to Delphi
for answers. Then,
on his return,

when I spoke with him first
his feet not yet on greeting terms
with home turf
the game was up:
the oracle had tugged
on the follicles of fate,

the Muses had met a mate;
spawned a poet,
under the meddling moon.

37.

the flexing sea
still lives in me, banished
to the body's byways;

I pass it
to smoke on contact
with the dust

this minor tributary
plays out history
in its disappearing act

will not carry goods,
freight; sinks
under its own weight

into the ground
that is not Earth
but the ashes

of its wishes
cast into space
to colonise a vacuum

38.

this morning
I'd swap my shield

for a sail
hand-sewn

for the pleasure
of being blown

39.

Neobulé, how
I have dreamed my sleep
away, drained

each drowsy drop,
hoping you're the source
of such moisture.

I'd travel
to where the tributaries
start as a trickle; tunnel

beneath the grazed knees
of raised hills
and cup what comes

to mouth

40.

you can hide
the Earth
under your thumb

like casualties vanish
in a puff
of statecraft

exfoliate
like the bad skin
of the moon

41.

in Hypnos's house
I roll fist-balls
into my body's pockets:

cave of knee-crook,
armpit's underworld.

In the morrow these hands
throb with warmth, fists
fall open like a flower-head

yet the fingers
are soon spiders: want
their dark haunt;

have planted eggs
in the recesses
unsure if they'll hatch

42.

Neobulé, may
the absent sea, still
bring you to me
on a skiff

through Hera's milk
'cross squid-inked skies
we hide in here; meet me

on imagin'd shores
where men slay Gods
for fuel

43.

the sparrow's beak
leaks no more song

and anyways
cannot fly for the mist

flung behind apple-pip eyes
robs him of direction

yet still there beats
deep in chest-nest

an uneven rhythm: hope's
insurrection

44.

blindness
less

to do
with the eyes

paralysis
of mind

enacted
upon the body

this prolonged
death at sea

45.

O big-hitting Zeus,
I call a truce: all
I now ask

is you ferment
this flask of dust and blood
under the month-long sun.

For if I cannot
be undone by drink, I may yet
be a source of it:

herein lie my wishes
slave-bread flat

46.

in the silence here
the body's an ear.

Through skin and hair
it hears
where nothing is sung

into pink holes
either side of the head;
craters

where once
all sound was flung

47.

courage, Glaucus
is no limb
protruding from six-packed trunks.

These men have such devices
and wield them
in conjunction with shield
and spear,

but here their infantry lesson
lessens in weight
for there is other mettle:

gravity lies
with the wise man
can put his dreams to sleep;

they need rest too,
will wake refreshed

and press their hands
into the soft clay
of your days

48.

of all citizens
of the ocean deep, creatures
that dart and dash
through my dreams,

I fear the nib
of the octopus' beak
hidden in the folds
'neath that fleshy bulb
of a head.

The eyes, gold-flecked,
vex me not; I've seen colder
in the market-place at Thrace
in the head of a creditor.

The arms hold
no trouble; I welcome
their wrap, am partial
to suction

49.

we moon-folk,
selenite citizens,
deliberate upon distance

for song
is a great attractor, hunter
and gatherer;

works the spaces
between Paros
and Thasos

traces how impulse
aches into action,
between limb-itch

and the poor fuck
whose luck it is
to receive the outcome

50.

we've reached
Mount Elsewhere,
given its dust
a good kicking

occasionally found
the black powder
turn to brown
when the sun crowns
certain shapes at noon;

for who forgets
we set forth
at the Sybil's urgent
invitation

for that moon
that haunts and hunts
the brushlands and borders
beyond;

where light plays
upon our sleep
and sounds it:
another song

of a different dawn
over the tall grain
we seek
that would not grow here

51.

Neobulé, in the heat
of your imaginary thighs

under the administrations
of your damp palms

all three of my eyes
stream

such fever
such a state

I'd happily participate in
true polis

52.

let's not jeer
at the dead; their bones
have a beauty and bounty

in their white witness
as tools of daily toils
happily discarded

as sword outwears sheath
and life passes
out through the teeth

53.

Lord Poseidon,
once I recall your wet-weave
netted a rippling moon
flexing yellow upon the Aegean

yet what possible jurisdiction
can you have here
where no horses ride
grey foam

yet we are submerged,
wits sink,
though all else
is light as an olive stone

54.

I'm less equipped
for Demeter's work
these lunar days,

and should I receive
a prompt
in my front
I'd be greatly surprised.

But build no bier:
step on me,
and I'll have more
than your foot

I bite deep
and lace
with dog bile.

55.

Glaucus, lick your finger
and taste
how we carry coast
on the skin

stranded on the crust
of the moon, with nothing
to dip it in
to make it soft.

So many blind eels
land-locked
away from the sea

56.

for what manner of shield
is a lyre; to what office
does it aspire

if not to protect
all prospects, sound
them in sinew and strum;

handle them
as a body bags jellied goods
in its skin-pouch

then wastes
through its holes what
it cannot keep

sings it out:
for song is a form
of passing

57.

Dionysus of the quickening
pulse, and pealing brain,
I remain your servant:

for you I'd do
the impossible, reinstate
the tyranny
of the lower body

here in the grey trenches
we've dug
in lunar mud
what foundations?

58.

a single boat
brought Lycambes' daughters
across the Styx.

A single note
carries no tune
through flute, 'cross lyre

it takes friction
to catch fire

59.

and what of our words
when the weight
has come off them

and Earth's a sapphire
set upon black;
this space

that comes between all
folk and things,
yet strings us along

beads at market
amongst the stars
and other gaseous bodies

60.

Zeus has a trick,
for once I saw it,
where he places the sun
in his pocket

and the light snuffs
like life can;
and in that blink
he played a message
down the horn of my spine

pure rhythm:
this dark song
to which I am given

61.

away from the sun
I sprout wishes
in the dark

as a picked beet
denies the pluck
and reaches for imaginary soil.

I groom these threads
with the honour
shown enemies in battle

when the field is settled
limbs scream
their last

and something for our leaders
bristles; a swallowed hair
you need to spit

62.

ah, little acorn,
  do you really suppose
great things might strain
  into being
from your shiny nub
  with tiny tip?

Even Demeter'd
  find it
an unlikely crop

63.

may she
who has loosened my knees,
tongue; and sits

on the urn of my chest
be blest with kindred ills;
I like to share

such trade
is iambic stock:
the broth of blame

64.

what regimen is a body
that head heaps
its orders on those below
yet Citizen Flesh contests;

from the red mess
a-slop in bone chest
to the outlying borders
there is chat

and that quickens
to a squall:
this struggle
to wisely govern an assembly

65.

Eros, relinquisher
of bodily ties,
below me lies the dust

I gently join,
skin revolting
flakes

spread above me
stars are salt
crystals on Zeus' black brow

66.

no groves, no
retirement to secluded shrines;
the moon
is a heap of stones

men add to
rock-by-rock,
leave their aches and weight
at the grey wayside

and here's the muddle:
this place is all middle,
we neither start nor end it.

Hermes, you lead,
herd us cattle
on the way across

67.

myths and legends
tell us much, yet fudge
certain issues.

Each day I am given
to recall Perseus's spoils:
that Gorgon's head
with the gift
of instant statuary;
how it was bagged,
and what happened to the bundle.

Humble Zeus, how
have you kept stumm,
hidden such planetary intervention?

Regale us with the tale
of your own beast fable;
that you stole this head of snakes
up into the dark of space,

rolled back the bag
from those onyx eyes,
aimed that fatal face
on your lunar prize:

the moon
turned to stone
finer than Parian marble.

How we chip at it now,
hope's quarry: tap at
the shape inside

68.

Glaucus, who'd have thought us
moon-mates on perpetual watch
for vital signs.

My own dwindle:
skin furrows and folds;
keeps moving with licence

that ill-becomes the young
—though I'm not yet fit
for a clay garment.

I am kin
to that big din of an Ox
with crumpled horn

who knows how to work
but chooses
not to.

69.

Neobulé, for what they say
my songs have done

I was banished to space
by a Delphic ruse
to found a city,

and found my body
a parchment map. Territory
of all you ever touched.

These marks
are the colonies I value,
where you landed

finger-tips, tongue
travelled
'cross rough brush,

wrinkled inclines, up
that raised area not climbed
in some time;

for I'm past that peak
and speak of it now
as an ex-citizen recast
as a bastard;

or as the sea
forgets its depths
strewn with lost property

70.

for you, Eros,
the body's a brawl
in a Thracian market place

unhinged, my limbs
lose their brotherhood, scrap
with the bunch
was once true company;

yet if this moon is ash,
it once was lit;
and even fighting men
search quick wits
for the semblance of a wick;

so here's the kick:
hope's that contrary prick
kindles fastest in the damp

71.

tomorrow
I'll send my fingers
to the surface of the moon

on a mission
to sweep debris, and creep
under Hecate's lid.

Yet we'll have
no simple burial; hands
you'll quarry deep

for clay, a wet
gray stuff so soft;
you'll drag this pulp

back, up to the top,
and under the spray of stars
we'll shape a jar,

delicate but deep; fire
this belly with desire-sparks
borne of my contest

with the dark chambers
of my heart.
And once it's baked

this vessel can wrestle
with my submission;
I'll take out

the seat of my rage
from its bone-cage
and squeeze.

A thick rain
will fall, carry
blame-clots,

bloody islands flushed
from my tributaries.
With these gone,

caught in this future jar,
I'll rest apart
from all I've pressed

into my art
like stained feet
after trodden grapes

72.

O guest-God, Zeus
finally I get it: when hope
loosens like ill-fitting cloth
you take it off, it itches;

so you've stripped us
and the skin sings
having shrugged off
the blue silk skies
for black space

and we admire the trick:
that you've stripped us bark
back to youngest wood,

and we saps on the moon
live in the grey of the Olive tree,
toughen like figs
in the drying sheds
on the shores of Paros

73.

dig Archilochus, dig!
scalp craters,
scrap and scrape;

take spear
and rake rocks
to powder;

deeper, down
into the underground;
it is here,
it must be, can't
rest

till you've found
all the moisture
you've wept

from eyes, pores
and much else;
all the water
you've dreamt

oceans of it
collect in caves
of prospect:
salt mines
on the moon

74.

belly, what of
your ever-emptying bowl;
why so full of holes,
when the body of a God
wastes not?

At times our soft outfit
blazes like warrior bronze
bouncing light
—till night arrests us

and we rivers run
downhill,
along the easiest paths;
and when blocked

we head for dark
underground, wind
round Earth's underside,
seeking gaps,
then gush like a mare
into the open day.

Gods don't leak
are sealed in constant light:
to us is given
the rhythm
of guttering torches.

75.

now I have recounted
my lunar tale
I shall compile
an inventory
of all that has been sent me
by the Gods,

chiefly
an ache
above and under
my left eye;
and one centred
between my thighs;

a hole
in the heart
I plug
with unmixed wine,
remains unfixed:
a song leaked
straight to my beak

76.

ok Neobulé,
I soften my position.

Take this rendition
as a token

you might swap
for a plot on the moon;

and when you get here
do something for me:

plant the seed of a whim,
harvest these hopes

so they live among us
ghosts of what we could be

77.

Neobulé, somehow
your space was deeper

full
as the promise of moisture

on the moon

78.

pitch this song
midways between yelp
and yearn;

may we all bare blame,
puckered like a goat's arse,
for its shoddy position;

share the task
of settling this camp
so far
from its promise

it can but point
forwards, pushed
so hard from behind

79.

when your ears sprout
  like stubborn veg
there's little doubting
  fate's gravity:

the weight of those strands.

I held her hand
  on Ionian sands
but I don't
  hold it now;

for this gray world
  is soft, but cold
and upon its craggy brow
  my songs fall old

all mind-dark.

80.

there are times
—the only waves here—
when I clear a path

through the brush
of my regrets
and accept that a man

can hate with a hope
for things
to be otherwise

the way a slave
forgets his master
in sleep

Grasping a Nettle Tongue: an Afterward(s)

I first discovered Archilochus in Herman Fränkel's *Early Greek Poetry and Philosophy*, and by chance became reacquainted via a charity shop copy of Guy Davenport's excellent *Thasos and Ohio* collection. History maintains that Archilochus was the first lyric poet, and in the ancient world he was second only to Homer in terms of poetic reputation. His is a nuanced voice, full of many tones and timbres—it tastes of brine, sweat, and handled coins; it has the viscosity of semen. It can argue and cajole, it can caress and curse. Viscosity is caused by friction; it is a measure of its resistance to gradual deformation. Archilochus crafted an "intimate yell" seven centuries before Christ, and a good many before Mayakovsky and Frank O'Hara. He was a soldier, part slave part aristocrat, who took part in the earliest colonial expeditions. His father, Telesicles, after consulting the oracle at Delphi, led the first colonising mission from Paros to Thasos. But he didn't venture to the oracle alone. His companion was Lycambes, who later agreed to the engagement of Archilochus and his eldest daughter Neobulé—and later, for reasons unknown, broke that arrangement.

I was intrigued by this ancient foundational moment of conjunction between lyric and colonization. To return to Archilochus is to understand that Lyric is territorial, it stakes claims; it desires to occupy, it forms an erotics of coercion. The skin of Archilochus's fragments (we have nothing complete) is pock-marked, uneven in tone, unwilling to entertain the promised idylls and abundance of colonial discourse. The lands he encounters are populated, there is friction. Civic crisis or personal trauma stimulates the colonial drive, and Carol Dougherty explains how a murderer's exile frequently "overlaps with the start of a colonial expedition". The exile I have established for this soldier-poet is steeped in the myths that surround him. Archilochus was famed for his metrical prowess and invention, and particularly for his association with Iambic verse. But this Iambic practice was no mere metrical observation. In Ancient Greece, Iambic verse was as much a question of subject matter;

it was a vehicle for ritual invective, obscenity, abuse and blame. And this raises interesting questions about the nature of Lyric practice. Whilst Archilochus is associated with a new flowering of personal investment in poetic utterance, critics have also raised the possibility that he speaks to us in vestments; that the voice is a rhetorical garment, "his song ... an artefact, not a vehicle for personal rage" (Anne Pippin Burnett). The names that litter and "authenticate" his verse, might also be types; "She who makes new plans" (Neobulé), "grey eyes" (Glaucos), "first sergeant" (Archilochus).

Carol Dougherty has explored in depth the ancient colonial narrative as "a Delphically sponsored solution to civic crisis at home", and has even pointed to how the decoding of riddling Delphic enigmas is akin "to the act of staking out territory settling new land". Archilochus's land here is the moon, that pock-marked shield in the dark that gleams unevenly; that curator of lost objects and desires, Jack Spicer's "big yellow eye remembering / what we have lost or never thought." What better impossible site upon which to locate the ageing poet's dissection of hope and desire, and his meditation upon the body that barely houses them. When Lycambes broke off the poet's engagement to Neobulé, legend has it that Archilochus wrote such scurrilous poems about the affair, that the entire family committed suicide. The basic premise to this book is that Archilochus has been sent—partly as punishment for the havoc his poems have wreaked upon Lycambes' family—into exile to colonise the moon.

These poems are not translations (though they owe so much to the translations of Guy Davenport and Michael Ayrton). They are occupations. I felt closest to Pound's 'Homage to Sextus Propertius', or Erin Mouré's *O Cadoiro*, where the poets have tuned into a frequency of lyric resistance, have captured a viscosity of voice; the friction of rubbing up against the recalcitrant fibres of everyday life in a time of war. Pound wrote his misunderstood Propertius during the first world war, to inhabit a voice so determined to resist the "large-mouthed product" of empire and propaganda. Erin Mouré, disgusted by

Bush-speak, sought to acquire another tongue; turning to the medieval Galician-Portugese *cantigas* enthralled by their breach with both "the epic narrative mode and with ecclesiastical modes of praise". Mouré values this lyric viscosity wherein the "speaker's own subjectivity, own feelings, are the poetic 'substance,' yet these are ... never 'unmediated', always social, intended, and profane: directed towards another human, not to God".

Selected Further Reading for the Curious

Michael Ayrton, *Archilochos*. London: Secker & Warburg, 1977.

Anne Pippin Burnett, *Three Archaic Poets: Archilochus, Alcaeus, Sappho*. London: Duckworth, 1983.

Guy Davenport, *Carmina Archilochi: the Fragments of Archilochos*. Berkeley, CA: University of California Press, 1964.

Carol Dougherty, *The Poetics of Colonization: From City to Text in Archaic Greece*. Oxford: Oxford University Press, 1993.

H.D. Rankin, *Archilochus of Paros*. Park Ridge, NJ: Noyes Press, 1977.

Michael Schmidt, *The First Poets: Lives of the Ancient Greek Poets*. London: Weidenfeld and Nicolson, 2004.

CPSIA information can be obtained
at www.ICGtesting.com
Printed in the USA
LVOW08s1550070217
523493LV00001B/183/P